This book is f

...you have become Suddenly Single th
you are looking for greater fulfilment a
life.

You're in a crisis and asking yourself, "What next?"

Having built a life and anticipated a future with your partner, are you on a path of uncertainty, both emotionally and financially?

Do you feel confident around money and have a trusted adviser who understands you?

Are you striving for fulfilment in later life?

Do you need help in reclaiming your identity, understanding your money and rebuilding your future?

If you can answer yes to any of these questions, this book is for you, so read on...

What people are saying about
Suddenly Single

*S*uddenly Single will act as your guide and empower you to fulfil your dreams. It will help you avoid common mistakes, ensure you feel supported and provide practical tips.

"When I first split up with my partner, my heart literally broke and I'd never knew pain like it, I thought I was going to die. The first few months I would walk to and from work crying, every night go to bed and cuddle my spare pillow feeling lonely and thinking I would never feel happiness again. I've been single now for over a year and my life has turned a full 360 degrees. Through the Suddenly Single Journey, I was able to take stock of my life and use that to move on. I've actually found happiness which I didn't even know existed. I am content about being on my own and have made peace with who I am and what I want from life. I have great family and friends and have filled my life with exercise and social events; it's actually going to take someone very special to give that up for. I now walk to and from work with a spring in my step and on a high."

Hannah

"Working with Jo through the Suddenly Single process has turned my finances around. When I thought I was in a black hole, she made it possible for me to see light at the end of the tunnel. Jo made me realise I was not on my own; her financial knowledge and insight allowed me to move forward in my life!"

Sue

This book uses real-life experiences and follows two fictional characters, Mary and Gwen, and their journey through the Suddenly Single Track.

About the Author

I have been a Financial Adviser for many years. I have loved every moment of it and get a real sense of satisfaction from helping people find more fulfilling lives, which extends far beyond the subject of money. If I could spend every day meeting and helping people, I would have found work utopia. I have a real passion for helping my clients get peace of mind, understanding and clarity around their money. But for me, it isn't just about the money – it is about what the money enables. My approach with clients enables empowered decision-making; giving them a life without fear of the future; gaining the confidence of independence and a feeling of liberation.

Importantly my approach overall enables suddenly single women to live the life **they** want to live again. How fabulous is that?! At last I feel I have found my purpose in life. To educate and inspire confidence in women regarding their monetary affairs, enabling them to be Happy, Healthy, Wealthy and Wise.

My clients are typically women who are suddenly single through divorce or bereavement. I too have found myself Suddenly Single but when I'm not advising clients, I lead a very fulfilling life, travelling, playing sport, keeping fit and keeping up with a very busy social life!

As a Fellow of the Chartered Insurance Institute, and a Suddenly Single female, I feel uniquely qualified to share my approach with others.

Find out more and visit the Suddenly Single website;
www.suddenly-single.co.uk

**So open your minds –
It's time to Take Stock, Take Charge and Take Off!**

When Life closes one door,
it opens another

Suddenly Single

Take Stock, Take Charge, Take Off

Jo Read

Published by

Filament Publishing Ltd

16 Croydon Road, Beddington, Croydon,

Surrey, CR0 4PA, United Kingdom.

Telephone +44(0) 20 8688 2598

www.filamentpublishing.com

© Jo Read 2016

ISBN 978-1-910819-27-2

Printed by IngramSpark

Table of Contents

Introduction

My life changed forever, on a flight to Vietnam several years ago. Well, technically, it changed before that, as I found myself in a situation I thought I'd never be in, Suddenly Single.

Happily married and building a life together with my husband, it all suddenly came crashing down when one day my husband told me he couldn't see himself spending the rest of his life with me. He'd made up his mind and nothing was going to change that, despite the tears, discussions, the trying to work out what went wrong along the way.

I went through all the emotions you can imagine – fear, loss, anger, guilt – but most of all I felt a failure. For anyone who knows me, that's about the worst thing that could happen to me. I'm successful, a Chartered Financial Planner, a Fellow of the Chartered Insurance Institute. I thought I was in control of my life, but then that moment came when I wasn't in control anymore. It unnerved me. It made me question everything about myself and my life. I had become Suddenly Single. And I didn't know what to do with myself.

As a Chartered Financial Planner, every day I come into contact with women who are going through what I went through. The majority of my clients are women who are Suddenly Single too, either through divorce or bereavement. I help these women take stock of their emotions, take charge of their finances, and help them to take off in their new life. There's a journey that I take them on, and that's what I love; giving women back that control, making them happier, healthier, wealthier and wiser, through a combination of financial planning advice, together with emotional support and guidance.

So, as I say, I found myself on a flight, getting away from it all. As you do, I struck up a conversation with the woman sitting next to me. It turns out that she was on a 'Thelma and Louise' type adventure with three friends. She had met them at a local hospice where, sadly, their partners had all died of cancer. She asked me what I did for a living so I told her. And before I knew it, I was telling her how I'd become Suddenly Single, much like my clients, and had taken this trip to take stock.

She told me of her own story, the difficulties she had faced trying to make her own way through the financial maze, not seeking advice and ending up not knowing which way to turn and what was best for her situation.

Unfortunately, her story was not unusual.

She turned to me and said, "People like you need to help people like us. You need to write a book for Suddenly Single people."

That was the defining moment. I knew what it was that I needed to do. My purpose was to educate and inspire confidence in Suddenly Single women, both emotionally and financially. I wanted to help them take control, so they'd be happier, healthier, wealthier and wiser.

And now you find yourself reading my book. I realised that what I was already doing with my clients on a daily basis could, and should, become a larger thing. I would be able to help more Suddenly Single women. Having gone through the experience myself, I was in a better position to understand what a huge life change this was. I am keen to build a Suddenly Single Community where Suddenly Singles can share experiences, get support, and have a place where they don't feel alone.

I formalised the process that I had been going through with my clients for many years, which now forms the Suddenly Single Journey:

Module 1 – Take Stock. This is where you consider 'where your head is emotionally'. There's no point trying to deal with the practical aspects unless the emotions are addressed. We look at the current situation, what needs to change, and what the end result looks like. We begin setting goals at this point and start to look into the future, turning negatives into positives.

Module 2 – Take Charge. This is where it gets into the nitty-gritty: how to get back on track and deal with the practical elements and finances. There's a client report and recommendations about how to move forward and understand what you have and what it can do for you. And then it's go, go, go!

Module 3 – Take Off! This is all about putting the plans into practice, and achieving the goals set in the previous module. I ensure everything's on track, and revisit three to six months down the line. If I need to tweak/update/re-evaluate at this point, I can do that. At the end of this module, all graduates should be fully in control of being Suddenly Single, and well on the way to their new life! Congratulations!

So what next...

The key to the Suddenly Single process isn't just about getting finances in order. It's about taking women through the emotional journey, providing support, understanding, and considering the bigger picture. The journey that I go on with my clients is about doing things in the context of what's right for them. For example, if it's the right time to up sticks and travel the world, I can help plan for that. If they want to sell their property or carry on living in it, I work out what the best solution is to help them achieve this and also to move forward and be content in this new life.

I want women to know that it's OK that there are many other women out there who have gone through this major life change. Yes, there's a lot of uncertainty, unknowns, and a feeling of failure. So, let's share those experiences and knowledge and build a Suddenly Single Community, a place for women to get support, share ideas and recommendations. I want to raise awareness of the Suddenly Single woman so they can connect with each other.

I want to share my process with as many Suddenly Single women as possible because it's helped many women turn their lives around and achieve things they never thought possible. I want to help women understand that Suddenly Single is a beginning, not an ending.

Where are you on the Happy, Healthy, Wealthy and Wise scale?

By the end of this book, I want you to be a 10 across all four!

Let's begin...

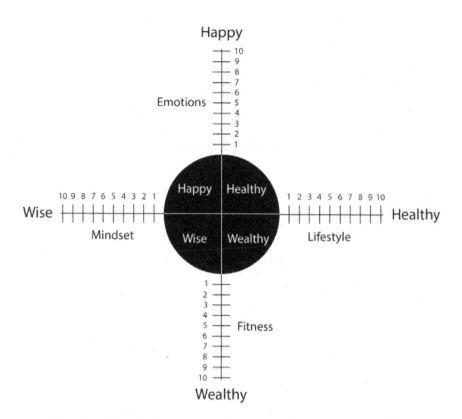

Download your copy of the Happy, Healthy, Wealthy and Wise scale
from the Suddenly Single website;
www.suddenly-single.co.uk

"Do the difficult things while they are easy and do the great things while they are small.

"A journey of a thousand miles must begin with a single step."

Lao Tzu

Chapter 1: What is the Suddenly Single Community and what do they need?

A *new force is silently sweeping our culture; a force that has already started to change the very fabric of how we organise our lives, how we relate to one another, how we use our money, our time, and our talents.*

This new force is the dramatic shift in the number of women who are single. This shift is a result of a new generation of divorcees and widows aspiring to redefine themselves. These Suddenly Single women will surge forward in an unending unfolding of new challenges, new opportunities, new options, and new discoveries.

Would it surprise you to know that a third of women live alone by the time they reach retirement age?

We all know someone who has become single due to divorce or bereavement. It is an emotional time for women and they are left asking themselves: what next?

Having built a life together as a couple, the anticipated future now looks uncertain, coupled with the daunting challenge of understanding your financial situation.

- *Can you afford to stay in your home?*
- *Will you have to continue to work, or go back to work?*
- *What sort of lifestyle can you lead?*

From research that has been carried out, one thing is very clear: women are incredibly resilient. They also showed that, irrespective of experience, women do not feel confident around money. Dealing with the unknown moves us out of our comfort zone; a place none of us choose to visit.

Striving for fulfilment in later life is one by-product of longevity. Over 50 is now affectionately known as Middle Adulthood. Liberation from menfolk may suit some women but for many it carries enormous hurt, vulnerability and loss of identity. It's a real fear for women. In particular, they are worried about:

- *How much money is enough?*
- *Will I meet anyone else?*
- *Will I still manage to fulfil my dreams?*

Working alongside family lawyers as a Chartered Financial Planner, I am well aware of the statistics. I too have become one of these stats!

Again, I recalled the words of my travelling companion on the flight to Vietnam.

"People like you need to help people like us. You need to write a book for Suddenly Single people."

But for me, it's more that I want to become part of a Suddenly Single Community, a place where I feel I belong, a special place I affectionately refer to as Suddenly Single Town.

I have created two fictional characters for this book based on real Suddenly Single experiences. They'll breathe life into the needs and wants of Suddenly Singles everywhere.

Taking back control is one major need, and I regularly ask my clients what it means to them. Here are some of their thoughts;

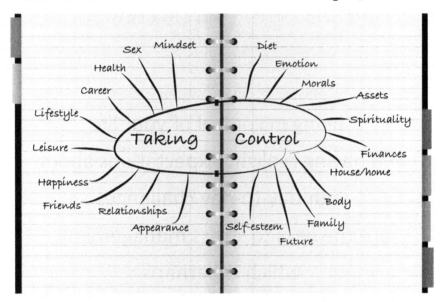

By following the book's framework, it is possible to feel in control again. Negative emotions can be transformed to:

- Positive emotions
- Interest
- Excitement
- Sense of control
- Ultimate peace of mind

Using Take Stock, Take Charge and Take Off as a central theme, the book aims to take you through three stages of discovery.

1. Take Stock – Where are you now?
2. Take Charge – Where do you want to be?
3. Take Off – How to get there.

These three stages will help you believe in yourself again, get tough and face the challenges, and use your common sense and intelligence in new ways to create a life that's Happy, Healthy, Wealthy and Wise.

"Being in control of your life
and having realistic expectations about
your day-to-day challenges
are the keys to stress management,
which is perhaps
the most important ingredient
to living a happy, healthy and rewarding life."

Marilu Henner

Chapter 2: You've just become Suddenly Single

Please allow me to introduce you to Mary and Gwen.

Mary and Gwen represent many women in the Suddenly Single Community: intelligent, hard-working women who once had flourishing careers that had to take a back seat so they could raise a family. They enjoyed a comfortable lifestyle managing their homes, whilst their husbands often took an active role in managing the family finances.

But now their world has changed and they're afraid and asking these fundamental questions:

- What next?
- How do I redefine myself and move on?
- Do I have enough money to maintain my lifestyle?
- Where can I get support and advice?

Mary's story

Mary had been married for 28 years to Richard, a good man, not exciting but reliable. Richard managed all the finances, the bills were always paid, they ran two cars, ate out regularly and went on holiday several times a year. A safe, predictable life that she was happy with. They had three children, two boys and a girl, and two adorable grandchildren. Mary worked part-time at the local school.

Richard had always worked long hours, and on reflection Mary had been very lonely. Filling her evenings the best she could, she went to the gym more frequently and created a great social life with the crowd from work. At home, she rattled around the house and the silence bounced off the walls. She had many photos and memories of the kids and grandkids having fun at home, but now she watched their lives and milestones on Skype or Facebook.

She hadn't seen it coming. One evening Richard had made it home on time and they settled down on the sofa with a glass of wine. He was agitated, nervous and was struggling to make eye contact.

"I don't know how to say this," he said, "but I've been feeling unhappy for a while. I love you but don't see a future with you."

Her heart raced, she was in total shock. She had suggested counselling but Richard didn't think this would help and said he needed to be alone to work through his feelings. Several weeks later, Richard moved out.

Mary's confidence was on the floor and at times she felt suicidal. Things hadn't been good in their marriage, but she still thought there was enough there to help them work through this bad patch. Mary believed marriage was for life. She had a very normal middle-class marriage, Richard worked and organised the finances and Mary stayed at home to look after the kids.

Mary's emotional equilibrium was destroyed. It felt as though she was trapped on a never-ending roller coaster:

- Anxiety – Can I cope alone?
- Fear – What impact will this have on my life? Can I keep the house?
- Happiness – Perhaps it's for the best... maybe I will be happier on my own?

But worst of all was the feeling of failure – could I have done differently? How could I have made him want to stay? What will I tell the kids? Mary found it hard to be alone; she felt unwanted, frumpy and old. She retreated in to her shell and didn't want to go out, but she felt she needed to take charge of her life. The first thing she decided to do was to understand her choices; could she stay in the house? Could she afford to rebuild her life? A friend recommended a financial adviser, Jo Read, who specialised in working with Suddenly Single women and helped them work through her Take Stock, Take Charge, Take Off track. Mary thought she had nothing to lose, so made an appointment to meet her.

Gwen's story

Gwen was only 54 when her husband Roy died. The couple had a daughter, who was in her early twenties. Gwen was Roy's second wife and had been married to him for 25 years. Roy had two children from his first marriage. He'd built a successful career and was CEO of a medical trust when he died. He'd also controlled all of the family finances.

Eighteen months before he passed away, Roy had been diagnosed with prostate cancer; he had completed a course of chemo and was in remission. The time before Roy passed away had been a difficult period of adjustment, but they had both been optimistic of a future together. Roy had semi-retired aged 58 and had organised the family finances to provide sufficient capital and income for them to enjoy their retirement. Gwen was still working as a nurse but had been considering taking a sabbatical to spend more time with her beloved husband.

The cancer diagnosis had devastated Gwen, while Roy had felt numb and unable to express any emotion or process any thought. When they heard the word cancer, the world greyed out for a moment, things seemed unreal, it was as though it was happening to someone else.

With Roy in shock, Gwen became responsible for taking in the details of the diagnosis and treatment. Roy just could not absorb the unexpected information.

She thought she needed to be there for him and not show her own feelings. But she too was adjusting to the fact that someone she loved had cancer. Her emotions changed day to day. There were periods of fear, anger, sadness and depression. At times she felt lonely and isolated and found it difficult to cope with the uncertainty of not knowing what may happen next. Then there was anger: why Roy? Why now? Getting angry does not mean you are a bad person – it just means you are having a hard time. But when anger goes on for a while, it can turn into resentment, especially when you are taking on more responsibilities. Gwen was trying to juggle a full-time job as well as supporting Roy. It seemed as if everyone only cared about Roy and didn't understand what she was going through.

Gwen needed support too and found some comfort in social media, and email. She regularly Skyped her daughter, who was in Australia; it was good to talk. If you can talk to just one other person about what you are going through, that may be the first step towards feeling better.

Sadness is a natural reaction when someone close to you is affected by cancer. You can feel sad all the time, or it might come and go.

People often feel sad when something disappoints them or when things change. The feeling of being powerless to change the situation is also upsetting. The loss triggered sad memories of when Gwen's mum had passed away. Her dad hadn't coped well and had got very depressed. Depression is more than feeling down for a few days, he was low for months; he struggled to cope with everyday life. Gwen had helped him find a support group which had done him a lot of good. Having people to talk to who are in the same situation can be a real help, a community like Suddenly Single where people support and share with each other.

When Roy left work, they were still optimistic that they would enjoy their retirement together. The plan was that he would do some consultancy for the NHS and Gwen would go part-time. Deep down though, Gwen believed Roy knew just how unwell he was.

Gwen became concerned when he started to get his affairs in order. He appointed a financial adviser who reviewed all their investments and pensions. Roy tried to involve Gwen but she was in denial and she didn't really pay attention, clinging instead to the hope that Roy would always be around to sort out their finances. That was the first mistake, as very suddenly Roy deteriorated. The doctor came to his bedside and informed them that Roy's condition was now terminal. Gwen wanted to be strong for Roy but her only thoughts were that her world had ended too.

Roy had been in the process of updating their wills but now he was too weak to focus. Gwen presumed that their old wills would be fine. Roy's last few days were spent in a hospice; the staff were amazing, anticipating their emotions and providing much needed comfort and support.

Roy passed away and Gwen's world became a haze. Her daughter came home from Australia and her strength helped Gwen take control of her life once again. She suggested the first thing to do was to arrange a meeting with their financial adviser, Jo Read. Roy had provided Jo with details of all their financials. Gwen knew she needed help to navigate through the money maze. And now it become apparent why Roy had chosen Jo as his financial adviser – she specialised in working with Suddenly Single women.

Gwen found the first meeting comforting. She wasn't alone, and several of the tips really resonated with her: write down your feelings, exercise and turn anger into assertiveness. She could visualise gradual acceptance and moving forward in accepting her Suddenly Single status. She wanted to become happier and healthier, to understand her wealth and to provide wisdom to others.

She scored herself on the HHWW scale and got a disappointing two!

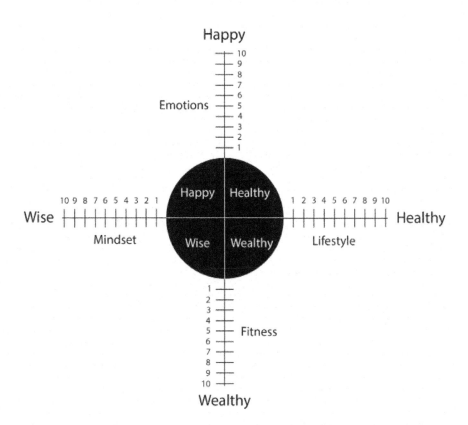

Chapter 3: Take Stock – Internalise

The first stage when Taking Stock is to really get to grips with where are you now. How do you feel? What's in the way and what's stopping you from moving forward?

This involves some deep soul searching, something that many struggle to do. Generally, internalisation is a long-term process of consolidating and embedding one's own beliefs, attitudes and values. This is one part of the Suddenly Single Journey that most people have difficulties with.

To support you on your journey, let me introduce you to three new concepts:

- **The Change Curve –** I like to refer to this as 'The Journey of Change'. This is a very useful tool to help your own understanding when managing personal change. Knowing where you are on the curve will help you decide how to communicate, what level of support you require and when best to implement change.
- **Start with 'Why' –** Simon Sinek[1] has written an incredibly powerful book on understanding your 'Why'. The book has a business slant but it also helps you understand your personal values, beliefs and why you do what you do.
- **Experience 'Your Best Year Yet' –** Jinny Ditzler[2] has created a really useful process to help you create your own action plan so that you can enjoy 'Your Best Year Yet'.

[1] *Start With Why: How Great Leaders Inspire Everyone To Take Action* by Simon Sinek (Penguin, 2011)
[2] *Your Best Year Yet!: Make the next 12 months your best ever!* by Jinny Ditzler (Harper Element, 2006)

The Suddenly Single Journey

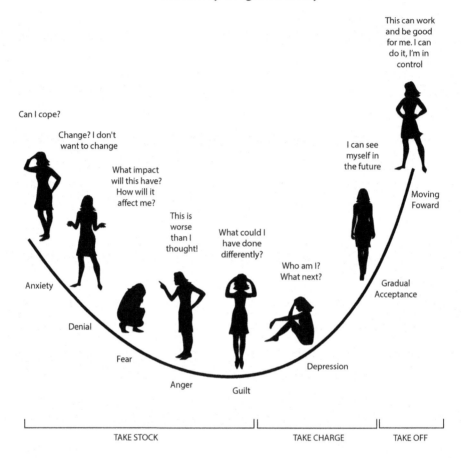

The Change Curve is based on a model dating back to the sixties and its purpose was to help people understand the grieving process. Since then it has been used as a method to help people understand their reactions to significant change or upheaval. The stages can be applied to any dramatic life-changing situation and include denial, anger, depression, bargaining and acceptance.

Stage 1 – Shock and Denial

The first reaction to change is usually shock. This initial shock, while frequently short-lived, can result in a temporary slow-down. People who are normally decisive seek more guidance and reassurance as they enter the realm of the unknown. When the initial shock has passed, it is common for people to experience denial.

At this point, the focus tends to remain in the past. You may want to avoid the situation as you are still confused. There are likely to be thoughts such as, "Everything was OK as it was, why me?" "Why did things need to change?" Common emotions include feeling threatened and that you have failed. You may feel numb and want someone to blame.

People who have not previously experienced major change can be particularly affected by Stage 1. It is common for people to convince themselves that the change isn't actually going to happen, or if it does, that it won't affect them. At this stage, communication is key so reiterate what the actual change is and the effects it may have. Provide reassurance too because that is vital.

Stage 2 – Anger

After the feelings of shock and denial, anger is often the next stage. A scapegoat is commonly found, passing the blame on to someone or something else allows a continuation of denial by providing another focus for fears and anxieties. Common feelings include scepticism, suspicion and frustration.

The lowest point of the curve comes when the anger begins to wear off and the realisation that the change is genuine hits. It is common for morale to be low, and for self-doubt and anxiety levels to peak.

Stage 3 – Depression

Feelings during this stage can be hard to express, and depression is possible as the impact of what has happened is acknowledged. This period can be associated with apathy, isolation and remoteness, as well as total detachment and a feeling of being overwhelmed. You may lack energy and feel helpless. The Change Curve underlines that these emotions are usual and shared amongst the Suddenly Single Community. There are lots of support groups that can help. These can provide a stable platform from which to move into the next stage of the Journey of Change. Groups to support you in this stage can be found on the Suddenly Single website: www.suddenly-single.co.uk

Stage 4 – Dialogue and Bargaining

During this stage, you will start to process what has happened. Often people struggle to find meaning in what has occurred and they begin to rationalise and debate. You may reach out to others and want to tell your story. This will help you regain control and begin to move on.

Stage 5 – Acceptance and integration

After the darker stages, 1 to 4, a more optimistic mood begins to emerge. People accept change is inevitable, and learn to work with the changes rather than against them. We start to think of exciting new opportunities, and there's great relief that you've navigated your way through the change. The final steps involve integration; the focus is firmly on the future and there is a sense that real progress has been made. The new situation has replaced the old and the feelings experienced are now acceptance, hope and trust.

Stage 6 – Empowerment

At this stage, you return to a meaningful life. You will feel secure again. You have regained your self-esteem.

YOU HAVE A FUTURE

Communication and support are still vital as it is not uncommon to return to an earlier stage if the support suddenly drops. Everyone reacts individually to change and will not experience every phase. Some people spend longer in Stages 1 and 2 whilst others move swiftly to Stages 4 and 5. There is no right or wrong way on this journey, there is only your way.

Mary shares her experience of her Journey of Change:

"When I reviewed the Change Curve, I decided that I had reached the anger phase. But it was much more than anger. I was frustrated and irritated with the situation that had been forced upon me. I would look at my friends and their happy lives, and get angry. Why hadn't their relationships failed? Then I'd feel embarrassed and ashamed for having these thoughts. I lacked energy and felt totally helpless. I needed to change.

"There are many support groups to help, but it took me a while to accept that I needed one. I always felt there was a taboo with joining a support group and I was reluctant to attend. But being part of the Suddenly Single Community, I found people to talk to. People who understood and shared their stories in return. With this support and the practical tips, I moved through the stages and decided to take charge... I did have a future.

"I actually started to feel empowered, my self-esteem returned and I started to reach out to others. I wanted to tell my story, to help others. I came up with a plan on my journey so that I could become Happy, Healthy, Wealthy and Wise. It helps to tell your story. You can share your story on the Suddenly Single website: www.suddenly-single.co.uk"

"Change is the only constant in life."
Heraclitus

Practical Tips

Stage 1

- Try to hear what is being said. Often when you are in shock, you have preconceived ideas and don't always hear what people are telling you. Write down some of your feelings. This can help to put things in perspective.
- Try to acknowledge emotions, whether they are yours or the other person's. Talk and be honest about them; don't ignore them.

Stage 2

- Talk about what's making you angry with someone else. You may find a solution by seeing things from a different point of view. Try to see the other person's perspective. Let the anger out (don't be afraid to do this, most people will be very forgiving at this time. Once you have let it out – let it go. It is healthier that way and it makes room for new emotions).
- Replace anger with assertiveness. This means saying what you think, feel and want, without criticising or blaming.

Stage 3

- Contact a counselling service. Talking about things in a more focused way with someone neutral can help you organise your thoughts and emotions. It will help put things in perspective.
- Do something to help your body and mind relax, such as slowing down your breathing, listening to music or meditation. Do some exercise. Even a short walk will release chemicals in your brain that make you feel happier. (See www.suddenly-single.co.uk for further information.)

Stage 4

- Keep talking; it's good to share. Tell your story. You are not alone. Surround yourself with positive people with shared experiences who can help you see you can move on.

Stage 5

- List all the positive things in your life, explore your options and put a new plan in place (more on this in the following chapters).

Stage 6

- Friendships. Real friends are for life; cherish them and never let them go. You have a future and it always improves when you share it!

Mary found her friends had been particularly important on her Suddenly Single Journey, as she explains;

"The right friendship is a rock for life; they don't just happen, you make them happen. I hadn't realised how important friends were until Richard had left.

"Richard had been my soulmate, my confidant, my comforter, my emotional and practical support. That friendship was now gone and I didn't know how to replace it.

"I had many friends but none that I felt very close too. Were they even real friends or were they just acquaintances?

"Real friends care about every domain in your life, physical, mental, your other relationships. They care about your thoughts and fears, they give honest opinions, they notice when you are upset, no matter how you try to hide it. You see them regularly and you feel totally comfortable to contact them for a deep and meaningful chat. They take initiative and make sacrifices to work on friendship. Mutual trust, respect, admiration, forgiveness and unconditional care, that's what real friends are.

"During the weeks after Richard left, I re-engaged with my friends and felt humbled by their support, loyalty and love. I did have real friends, friends who were loyal and non-judgemental, friends who let me be a mess. They'd turn up on my doorstep late at night with wine and Kleenex.

"I hadn't worked hard enough on my friendships, but now I'm Suddenly Single, this has changed. I make time to be 'a Real Friend'."

"The friend who can be silent with us
in a moment of despair or confusion,
who can stay with us in an hour
of grief and bereavement,
who can tolerate not knowing...
not curing, not healing...
that is a friend who cares."

Henri Nouwen

Start with Why

Start with Why by Simon Sinek is a book for those who want to inspire others or for those who want to find someone to inspire them. This book has been recommended to me by many people, and after reading it, I can understand Why! It helps you understand who you are and why, it helps you find meaning. If we start with the wrong questions, if we don't understand the cause, then even the right answers will always steer us wrong. This book has many themes and those I find most inspiring are:

- **The Golden Circle** – This principle helps us understand why we do what we do. The part of our brain that controls our feelings has no capacity for language. It is this disconnection that makes it so hard to put our feelings in to words. We have trouble, for example, explaining why we married the person we married and why we love them, so we rationalise it; he's funny, he's smart. Yet there are lots of funny and smart people in the world and we don't love them or want to marry them. This is where gut decisions come from, they just feel right. But they don't come from the gut at all, just the limbic part of the brain. The Golden Circle helps you find clarity, discipline and consistency.

- **The Emergence of Trust** – When we share values and beliefs with others, we form trust. Trust of others allows us to help protect ourselves and our children, and ensures our personal survival. Trust is a remarkable thing. Trust allows us to rely on others for advice and to help us make decisions. It is the bedrock for the advancement of our own lives and our families. Whom do you trust more: someone you know or someone you don't? What do you trust more: a claim in a piece of advertising or a recommendation from a friend? We trust the judgement of others; personal recommendations go a long way, particularly from those who share our beliefs and values.

Gwen found this book particularly helpful. She explains why;

"Having spent more than two decades with Roy, I found this book a revelation. Many of my beliefs and values had been influenced by Roy. This hadn't been intentional, perhaps it just felt easier at the time. Finding my 'Why' has inspired me to take up new hobbies such as Tai Chi and it's expanded my travel horizons. I was always more of a risk-taker than Roy and now I'm going to indulge it and explore Asia with friends."

Practical Tip

You can learn so much from reading new books. Have a look at our recommended book list on *www.suddenly-single.co.uk*

Experience 'Your Best Year Yet'

This book, by Jinny Ditzler, is another great book to help you through your Suddenly Single Journey. I first came across it more than 10 years ago when the company I worked for used it to help us set goals. I now use this book and process on an annual basis with a group of friends. Working through *Your Best Year Yet!* can transform how you feel and all that is important to you. It is designed to reach the core of how you think and what you want to achieve, and will empower you to new levels of effectiveness and fulfilment. On this journey of self-discovery, it allows you to stand back, take stock and plan. The most important lesson is to take the time to review what is important to us in our lives.

Mary summarises her experience of following *Your Best Year Yet*.

"Successful businesses set goals, so why don't we? Following the Best Year Yet track made me see that I wasn't living the way I wanted to, I wasn't being true to myself. It helped me stop postponing a lot of things that are dear to me. I always used to consider myself strong and capable, but recently I'd been consumed by pain, wondering what was wrong with me and why there wasn't one person in the world to love me and share my life. I didn't want to be alone.

"After following the stages of the Change Curve; I accepted my emotions and understood I needed to reclaim my dreams. I'd diminished as a person and lost the ability to make changes. I told myself that's just the way it is, mustn't grumble. The idea of even setting a goal such as putting the romance back in my life didn't occur to me anymore. I'd built up a defence mechanism and couldn't stand the thought of trying another relationship and failing again. I'd gradually become a passenger in my own car never finding time to take stock

"Your Best Year Yet forced me to get out of the car and take a good long look at my life!"

Practical Tip

How do you feel now? Where are you on the Journey of Change? Download and print the Journey of Change from the Suddenly Single website. Put the copy somewhere you can see it every day, to remind you...

YOU HAVE A FUTURE

The Journey of Change

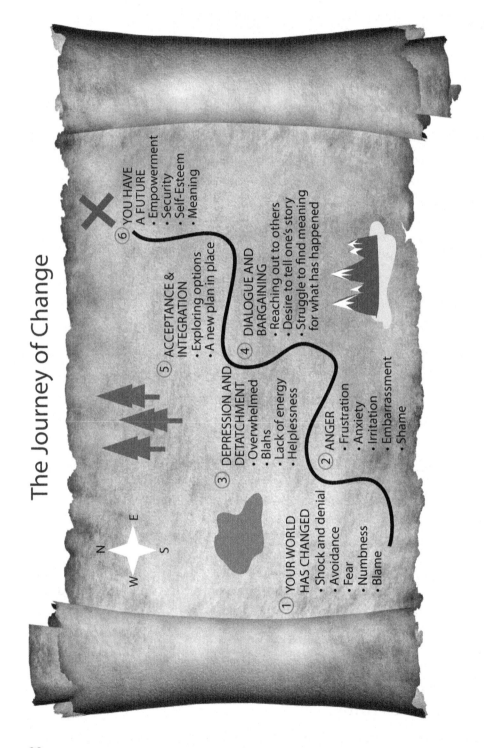

N
W E
S

① YOUR WORLD HAS CHANGED
- Shock and denial
- Avoidance
- Fear
- Numbness
- Blame

② ANGER
- Frustration
- Anxiety
- Irritation
- Embarrassment
- Shame

③ DEPRESSION AND DETATCHMENT
- Overwhelmed
- Blahs
- Lack of energy
- Helplessness

④ DIALOGUE AND BARGAINING
- Reaching out to others
- Desire to tell one's story
- Struggle to find meaning for what has happened

⑤ ACCEPTANCE & INTEGRATION
- Exploring options
- A new plan in place

⑥ YOU HAVE A FUTURE
- Empowerment
- Security
- Self-Esteem
- Meaning

Your Best Year Yet focuses on 10 questions and aims to help you acknowledge and appreciate what happened in the previous year. it also helps you define useful lessons and create a positive internal focus for producing results. You'll identify your top 10 goals and learn a system of planning to ensure success and happiness.

1. What did I accomplish last year?
2. What were my biggest disappointments?
3. What did I learn?
4. How do I limit myself and how can I stop?
5. What are my personal values?
6. What roles do I play in my life?
7. Which role is my major focus for next year?
8. What are my goals for each role?
9. What are my top 10 goals for next year?
10. How can I make sure I achieve my goals?

When Mary was asked question 1, this was her response:

"So what did I achieve last year?

"Nothing was my initial response, but on reflection some things had happened that I felt good about.

"I'd made several close friends at the support groups. I went back to work full-time at a job that I loved.

"I joined a gym and lost three kilos. Once I started, I couldn't stop."

"To be yourself in a world
that is constantly trying
to make you something else
is the greatest accomplishment."

Ralph Waldo Emerson

Mary continued to question 2...

"What were my biggest disappointments?

"This list was easy:

- *I'd endured a traumatic separation.*
- *I'd put all my travel plans on hold.*
- *I'd lost the person I shared my life with.*

...and the list went on. Writing all of these things down made me realise, what happens, happens, the only thing I can control is how I respond to it. I needed to stop feeling like a failure; this was weighing me down like excess baggage and I needed to stop driving while continuously looking in the rear-view mirror."

"We must accept finite disappointment,
but never lose infinite hope."

Martin Luther King, Jr.

Mary continued...

"What did I learn?

- *I learned that you can't make someone love you, a painful lesson.*
- *Feeling like a failure is very destructive on your life.*
- *I am resilient and not alone in how I am feeling.*

"Life is a classroom, we are always learning and need to heed the lessons that we have learned. I can turn these lessons in to personal guidelines."

Practical Tip

Complete questions 1, 2 and 3.

1. What did I accomplish last year?
2. What were my biggest disappointments?
3. What did I learn?

"Out of your vulnerabilities

will come your strength."

Sigmund Freud

Chapter 4: Take Stock – Envision

Your goals... our guidance

**The definition of envision is to
'Imagine a future possibility', 'mentally picture...'**

The next stage in Taking Stock is to look at where you want to be.

Many found this part of the Suddenly Single Journey very exciting. I believe that anything you want to do is possible. We are now much more independent than our mothers' generation. We are keen to learn new skills and experience new things. The world has become a much more accessible place, and what's wrong with wanting to explore and experience more in our lifetimes?

Envision encourages you to look forward and visualise the future. We've all heard the phrase 'where would you like to be in five or ten years' time?' but few of us ever take time out to truly picture what good looks like.

Let's take some time to do that now;

Utilising *Your Best Year Yet* as a starting point, let's consider several more questions:

- How do I limit myself and how can I stop?
- In which areas of my life am I not achieving what I want?
- What are my personal values?
- What are my goals?
- What do I want to do for fun?

We love our limitations; we must because we certainly don't want to let them go. There is always someone or something else to blame; our limitations become a habit.

Gwen considered these questions:

How do I limit myself and how can I stop?
"I've been feeling like a victim for some time now: 'why me?', 'why now?' I'd been allowing my victim status to limit me to thinking I could never have it all again, or be happy. Those around me seem to have it all. Why can't I have a career, family, fun and an optimistic future? I'd never really taken time to understand what was important to me. Discovering what was holding me back helped uncover the doubts and fears and erase the negative effects these were having on me."

In which areas of my life am I not achieving what I want?
"I feel as if I'm not in control of my own destiny and I've not planned ahead or taken control. I'd like to feel more in control of my finances. I'd like to get fitter and travel more and use my creative side. I need to allow myself to think about new possibilities and become enthusiastic about my future."

What are my personal values?
Gwen thought long and hard about this question and produced her list:
1. *"I believe that you are in control of your happiness – circumstances don't create our happiness and contentment, that's our job.*
2. *I believe in being healthy and taking care of myself.*
3. *I like to try new things and self-improve.*
4. *I like to support and improve the quality of life for my family and friends."*

What are my goals?

"I hadn't set any goals for many years; Roy and I had often done the same things, holidayed in the same places, eaten in the same restaurants. But they do say people who have goals achieve more in their lives. With this in mind, I went about setting specific goals linked to my values and came up with a list and action plan:

1. *To feel happy, positive and content – write down daily all the things that have gone well today. Recognising my Little Wins should increase my positivity and happiness.*
2. *To be healthy and self-improve – do a form of aerobic exercise three times a week. This will help me lose weight, give me more energy and improve my health.*
3. *Enjoy more time with friends and family – I will enrol on a course on social media and modern technology. This will help me connect and stay in touch with friends and family more easily."*

Practical Tip

Spend time alone or with friends working through the remaining questions. These can be found at www.suddenly-single.co.uk with supporting material.

In the quest to envision and imagine the future, a useful habit to form is to begin with the end in mind. What does your future look like?

For me, it's to be Happy, Healthy, Wealthy and Wise (HHWW). This will mean different things to different people.

Practical Tip

Take time to consider what HHWW means to you.

Mary shares her thoughts:

"HAPPY — waking up every morning and wanting to get up and embrace the day. Doing a job I love, spending time with the people I care about.

"HEALTHY — staying in shape and trying new activities

"WEALTHY — having a simple life but having enough money to do the things I want

"WISE — understanding my Why and what I want to get out of life."

Understanding and forming effective habits can help in shaping our HHWW outcomes.

A book worth reading is *The 7 Habits of Highly Effective People* by Stephen Covey[1].

1. Be proactive
2. Begin with the end in mind
3. Put first things first
4. Think win-win
5. Seek first to understand before being understood
6. Synergise
7. Sharpen the saw

[1] *The 7 Habits of Highly Effective People* by Stephen R. Covey (Simon & Schuster UK, 2004)

I have summarised each habit and believe these are all important to the Suddenly Single woman and her journey to a better future.

Habit 1 – Be proactive. Your life doesn't just happen. Whether you know it or not, it is carefully designed by you. The choices, after all, are yours. You choose happiness. You choose sadness. You choose decisiveness. You choose ambivalence. You choose success. You choose failure. You choose courage. You choose fear. Just remember that every moment, every situation, provides a new choice. And in doing so, it gives you a perfect opportunity to do things differently to produce more positive results.

Habit 2 – Begin with the end in mind is based on imagination, the ability to envision in your mind what you cannot at present see with your eyes. It is based on the principle that all things are created twice. First there is a mental creation, and then a physical creation. The physical creation follows the mental, just as a building follows a blueprint. If you don't make a conscious effort to visualise who you are and what you want in life, then you empower other people and circumstances to shape you and your life by default. It's about connecting again with your own uniqueness and then defining the personal, moral, and ethical guidelines within which you can most happily express and fulfil yourself. **Begin with the end in mind** means to begin each day, task, or project with a clear vision of your desired direction and destination. You create your own destiny and secure the future you envision.

Habit 3 – Put first things first. To live a more balanced existence, you have to recognise that not doing everything that comes along is OK. There's no need to overextend yourself. All it takes is realising that it's all right to say no when necessary and then focus on your highest priorities. It is about life management – your purpose, values, roles, and priorities. What are 'first things'? First things are those things you, personally, find of most worth. If you put first things first, you are organising and managing time and events according to the personal priorities.

Habit 4 – Think win-win isn't about being nice, nor is it a quick-fix technique. It is a character-based code for human interaction and collaboration. Most of us learn to base our self-worth on comparisons and competition. We think about succeeding in terms of someone else failing – that is, if I win, you lose; or if you win, I lose. There is only so much pie to go around, and if you get a big piece, there is less for me; it's not fair, and I'm going to make sure you don't get anymore. We all play the game, but how much fun is it really? Many people think in terms of: either you're nice or you're tough. Win-win requires that you be both. It is a balancing act between courage and consideration. To go for win-win, you not only have to be empathic, but you also have to be confident. You not only have to be considerate and sensitive, you also have to be brave. To do that, to achieve that balance between courage and consideration, is the essence of real maturity and is fundamental to win-win.

Habit 5 – Seek to understand before being understood. Communication is the most important skill in life. You spend years learning how to read and write, and years learning how to speak. But what about listening? What training have you had that enables you to listen so you really, deeply understand?

If you're like most people, you probably seek first to be understood; you want to get your point across. And in doing so, you may ignore the other person completely, pretend that you're listening, selectively hear only certain parts of the conversation or attentively focus on only the words being said, while missing the meaning entirely. So why does this happen? Because most people listen with the intent to reply, not to understand. You listen to yourself as you prepare in your mind what you are going to say, the questions you are going to ask, etc. You filter everything you hear through your life experiences, your frame of reference and consequently, you decide prematurely what the other person means before he/she finishes communicating.

Habit 6 – Synergise. To put it simply, synergy means 'two heads are better than one'. Synergise is the habit of creative cooperation. It is teamwork, open-mindedness, and the adventure of finding new solutions to old problems. But it doesn't just happen on its own. It's a process, and through that process, people bring all their personal experience and expertise to the table. Together, they can produce far better results that they could individually. It is the idea that the whole is greater than the sum of the parts. Valuing differences is what really drives synergy. Do you truly value the mental, emotional, and psychological differences among people? Or do you wish everyone would just agree with you so you could all get along? Many people mistake uniformity for unity; sameness for oneness. Differences should be seen as strengths, not weaknesses. They add zest to life.

Habit 7 – Sharpen the Saw means preserving and enhancing the greatest asset you have – you.

You've probably heard the expression...

"Insanity = Doing the same thing over and over again, and expecting different results."

Albert Einstein

It's amazing how quickly we can fall into bad habits. It's easy to stick to things that are familiar and find excuses about why things can't be different.

But if you keep doing things the way you've been doing things, you'll keep getting the same results;

- Unhappy relationships
- Passionless work
- Extra pounds
- Financial uncertainty
- Low self-esteem
- Disconnect from family

If you want things to change, if you want different results in your life, what you need to do is very simple.

Stop viewing your life through the rear-view mirror and create new habits for success.

Practical Tip

Create a list of the specific things/circumstances you want to be different in your life. Write down what behaviours or habits you engage in that are getting you the result you don't want. Then, *go out of your way* to do things differently. Give yourself permission to drive with your eyes firmly ahead.

"If you do what you've always done, you'll always get the same results."

Anthony Robbins

'Begin with the end in mind' –
Envision what you want in the future
so that you know concretely what to make a reality.

Mary enjoyed **Habit 2** and shares her thoughts:

"I found this habit particularly engaging. Thinking ahead and planning my future had been something I'd found very daunting. But being encouraged to think about all the things I wanted to do, to envision it all was actually liberating. I spent a couple of hours with my friends over a bottle of wine constructing my bucket list.

"To be honest, I wasn't really sure what a bucket list was and why I needed one. If you don't know what a bucket list is either, it is just a list of all the goals you want to achieve, dreams you want to fulfil and life experiences you want to have before you die.

"OK, I hear some of you say, I understand what it is but why do I need one? It seems like a lot of effort.

"Let me explain its power.

"If you don't live your days by personal goals and plans, chances are you spend most of your time caught up in a flurry of day-to-day activities. Ever feel your days are passing you by without anything really happening, like Groundhog Day? What did you accomplish in the past three months? What are your upcoming goals for the next three months? Look at the things you did and the things you're planning to do next: do they mean anything to you if you were to die today? Having a bucket list reminds you of what's really important so you can act on them.

"It's a place to set down anything and everything you've ever wanted to do, whether it's big, small or random.

"It's just like planning ahead all the highlights you want for YOUR whole life. I found many new things to do while I was writing my own list. It was an incredibly insightful exercise. What's more, coming up with my list gave me a whole new layer of enthusiasm knowing what's in store ahead!

"My list consisted of 60 new things to do before I was 60; there was still more work to do but I was pleased with the list so far. My friends and I cried with laughter discussing all the things we would like to do, and some were not fit to be listed in this book! The final list was a combination of activities, places to visit, health and beauty treatments, and challenges."

An example of Mary's bucket list

- Walk the Thames
- Adopt an animal
- Spend some time working in a charity shop
- Have a fish pedicure
- Try hot yoga
- Go to the polo
- Try acupuncture or alternative health treatments
- Ride a tandem
- Climb a mountain/three peaks challenge
- Go to a jazz club
- Dine in the dark at Dans Le Noir
- Spend the day with a personal shopper/stylist
- Go to a sporting event overseas
- Go to an IMAX cinema
- Play a game of golf
- Visit Costa Rica
- Give blood
- Go to the opera

Practical Tip

Spend time creating a bucket list. Don't let the weeds grow around your dreams, get gardening!

Envision is about setting goals and things to look forward to. Doing the exercise will give you the confidence to pursue your dreams.

Check out some bucket list ideas on the Suddenly Single website; www.suddenly-single.co.uk

Chapter 5: Take Stock – Negative to Positive

When we take responsibility for our capacity for positive change, we can control and guide our intelligence and our feelings, and point them towards the results we want. As this happens, we are drawn towards our goals as if by a magnet.

Rebalance your perception of yourself; if you start by thinking about the good news, you'll be in far better shape to make it happen. Almost without exception, people's initial thoughts about the past are negative, our consciousness is snared by bad news and the things we didn't get done. Start with a pat on the back.

It is time to establish what is in the way and stopping you moving forward. It is time to leave all your negative baggage and move in to positive territory.

It's time to...

Forgive, forget and learn

Mary had found it particularly hard to apply these words to her life as explained:

"I had found it very difficult to forgive, forget or move forward.

"Understanding the Change Curve (covered in Chapter 2) had really helped me to visualise where I was and that I had struggled to move past the anger phase. The Change Curve helped underline that these emotions are expected. I felt I had now replaced anger with

assertiveness, but every now and again the anger returned. I knew that my negative thoughts had really affected my self-esteem.

"I knew I must replace these lingering negative thoughts with positive ones if I wanted to become a Happy, Healthy, Wealthy and Wise woman."

Our idea of a wise woman is one who leads the way on several levels;

She leads the way at a personal level, creating a supportive environment in which she as an individual can flourish: physically, mentally and spiritually. It's a way of thriving where she can say yes to life while also saying no to guilt, no to burnout and no to other people's expectations.

She leads the way at a family level, cultivating conditions for health, happiness and harmony.

She leads the way at the levels of work and community, nurturing groups and building friendships that value respect and support.

To become a wise woman, you need to understand the negativity that holds you back. There is actually quite a lot of theory around why we behave the way we do and although I am no expert, I have found it easier to understand and have a more positive outlook now my 'monkeys' are under control.

Let me explain.

There are three parts of the brain that we need to understand. Our lizard brain, our monkey brain, and our human brain.

The 'lizard brain' is found at the base of the brain, and contains the cerebellum and the brainstem. Lizards only have these elements of the brain, which controls our most basic instincts. It is also sometimes known as the reptile part of the brain. It is the survival part that has you see the world as a dangerous place where most people and most things can't be trusted.

Its main purpose is to make sure that you can escape and survive any dangerous or stressful situation.

The next part of the brain, the 'monkey brain', includes the majority of our tissue, and controls more complex tasks as well as emotions. Most mammals lead with their 'monkey brain', which is fuelled by our most basic responses to fear and desire. This is the functional part of your brain that has you see the world as a set of challenges and problems for you to play with and explore while you ride the emotional highs and lows that they make you feel.

The most advanced part of the brain is the 'human brain', which consists of the outer layer, surrounding the 'monkey brain'. This area allows for logical, emotionless thought, as well as delayed gratification. It is by using our 'human brain' that we are able to think through our responses, rather than just reacting. Sometimes also known as the Empire Builder part of the brain, it is the humanitarian part which has you see the world as a deeply connected place that you can transform in a meaningful way.

But, when we are faced with threats to our system, we don't have time to stop and analyse what's going on. During these times we are glad to have our 'lizard' and 'monkey' brains get us to safety through our fight or flight response.

Because we have so many things going on at one time, when we multitask we can easily find ourselves using our 'monkey brain', making the wrong decisions that may end up causing serious problems with important tasks, or even worse, with important relationships.

Next time you find yourself trying to do a million things at once and getting irritable or grumpy with someone you care about, remind yourself that you're using your 'monkey brain', and work on acting more like a human.

We need to learn to tame our monkeys!

Tame your monkeys

Smart people have been teaching us about the human brain for more than 2,500 years about the human mind, so that we might understand ourselves better and discover a way out of suffering. The human brain can be described as being filled with wild monkeys, jumping around, screeching, chattering, and carrying on endlessly. We all have monkey minds, with dozens of monkeys all clamouring for attention. Fear is an especially loud monkey, sounding the alarm incessantly, pointing out all the things we should be wary of and everything that could go wrong.

Many believe meditation can help tame the wild monkeys in their minds. It's useless to fight with the monkeys or to try to banish them because, as we all know, that which you resist persists. You can, over time, tame the monkeys. Meditation is a wonderful way to quiet the voices of fear, anxiety, worry and other negative emotions.

For thousands of years, meditators have claimed many benefits for their practice. Research suggests that regular mindfulness practice, through meditation, is an effective treatment for stress, worry, lack of focus, relationship problems, addictions and more.

Gwen found this session particularly helpful and went on to explain more details around the monkey theory. Let her tell you how she deals with her monkeys...

"I can remember how satisfying it was when I first realised I had monkeys. That may sound strange but I felt comfort in the fact that it wasn't me; I wasn't this negative, glass half-empty person. I just spent too much time listening to them. I was recommended a book called The Chimp Paradox[1]. I read with interest and recommend you read it too.

"The chimp and monkey are used as a metaphor representing an emotional machine that thinks independently from us. It is not good or bad, it is just a monkey.

"You are not responsible for the nature of your monkey but you are responsible for managing it.

"One of the secrets of success and happiness is to learn to live with your monkeys and not get bitten or attacked by them. To do this, you need to understand how your monkeys behave, and why they think and act in the way they do. You also need to understand your human part of the brain and not muddle up your human self with your monkey.

[1] *The Chimp Paradox: The Mind Management Programme to Help You Achieve Success, Confidence and Happiness* by Prof. Steve Peters (Vermilion, 2012)

"I had always wanted to try meditation and when I realised it would help tame my monkeys, I signed up for a course. I now follow a daily ritual, usually at night when I find it difficult to sleep.

"Meditation produces a clearing of the mind in ways that promote a sense of calm and heightened awareness.

"It leads to peace of mind and well-being, greater focus and creativity and better relationships. There are many techniques used in meditation as a means to develop positive inner qualities and to transform negative ones. I have found meditation a huge help in making me more positive about my future.

"Engaging the monkeys in gentle conversation can sometimes calm them down. Fear seems to be an especially noisy monkey. As the months pass, my Fear Monkey shows up less and less, but when he does, he's always very intense. So I take a little time out to talk to him. He recently showed up when I thought about setting up a small business, growing flowers for weddings."

"You don't want to set up your own business!" Fear Monkey said.

"What's the worst that can happen?" I asked him.

"You'll go broke," he said.

"OK, what will happen if I go broke?"

"You'll lose your home," the monkey answered.

"Will anybody die if I lose my home?"

"Hmmm, no, I guess not."

"Oh, well, it's just a house. I suppose there are other places to live, right?"

"Uh, yes, I guess so."

"OK then, can we live with it if we lose the house?"

"Yes, we can live with it."

By the end of the conversation, Fear Monkey is still there, but has calmed down.

Learning to manage your monkey mind is one of the best things you can do to transform fear. Pay attention to how your monkeys act – listen to them and get to know them, especially the Fear Monkey. Learn how to change the conversations in your head.

Practical Tip

Engage your monkeys in conversation.

Turning negative thoughts in to positive thoughts is a really important part of the Suddenly Single Journey.

We human beings have an enormous capacity to remember our failures while forgetting our successes. The memory of our failures causes us to lower our sights and lessen our opinion of ourselves. It's easy to feel let down by failed resolutions; weight not lost, miles not run, friends not seen, cupboards not cleaned.

Everybody does it, but it's time to stop. One of the techniques I use to help promote positive thoughts is something called;

'Little Wins'

Little Wins helped me to recognise and embrace my successes.

The Little Wins exercise will help in removing negative things you do and make you focus and verbalise the positive things you do.

Success and positivity are made up of lots of Little Wins. A little win is a concrete, complete, implemented outcome of moderate importance. By itself, one little win may seem unimportant. Little Wins are controllable opportunities that produce visible results.

Once a little win has been accomplished, forces are set in motion that favour another 'Little Win'. Little Wins build people's confidence, positivity, and reinforce their natural desire to feel successful. A series of Little Wins therefore provides a foundation of stable building blocks. Each win preserves gains and makes it harder to return to pre-existing conditions; each win also provides information that facilitates learning and adaptation. Little Wins focus on the here and now.

Q: How do you eat an elephant?
A: One bite at a time!

Each bite we take of the proverbial elephant represents progress – a 'Little Win' – toward the larger, more significant goal. There's always some progress to recognise, even on the most challenging or discouraging days.

Practical Tip

First thing in the morning, fill in a daily calendar entry, email, text, or tell someone about your Little Wins from the day before.

Here is an example:

"Monday Wins: left the car at home and walked to work, had a healthy food day, put a deposit down on a new car, good deed gave my friend a lift to the airport, resolved a problem at work."

Mary loved Little Wins and had embraced the daily ritual.

"It's easy; I've set up a Suddenly Single WhatsApp and Twitter account so we can all share our Little Wins. Initially it was hard to think of wins from the day before, some days I would post I've got nothing! But now they are free-flowing and every day I can think of lots of things to post. Equally I love to hear about my friends' Little Wins.

"This was my post today:
Monday Wins: Ease back into fitness session with personal trainer, good planning meeting at work, nice dinner out with friends I haven't seen for a while."

Practical Tip

Set yourself a calendar entry for Friday evening and toast the wins from the week, discuss them with a friend, then look forward to and visualise the wins you would like to achieve next week.

Remember, human beings have an enormous capacity to remember our failures while forgetting our successes. Friends are vital to your Suddenly Single Journey. Spend time with them sharing Little Wins and Friday Toasts.

It's time to TAKE STOCK about where you are on the HHWW scale.

HAPPY – You've re-engaged with your friends. You are rebuilding your network for support and fulfilment. You are sharing your Little Wins and Friday Toasts. You understand the Journey of Change that you are on and you can start to see that you do have a future.

HEALTHY – You've evaluated your health and lifestyle and set goals. You've opened your mind to trying new things such as meditation. You've completed a bucket list to include new experiences.

WEALTHY – There is still work to be done on this scale but you have considered your values and set goals. You will need to map your wealth to your bucket list but now have some idea of what this looks like.

WISE – You know the right questions to ask yourself to have 'Your Best Year Yet'. You understand your 'Why' and the habits of effective people. You understand your monkeys and how to tame them!

Why don't you take time to score yourself?

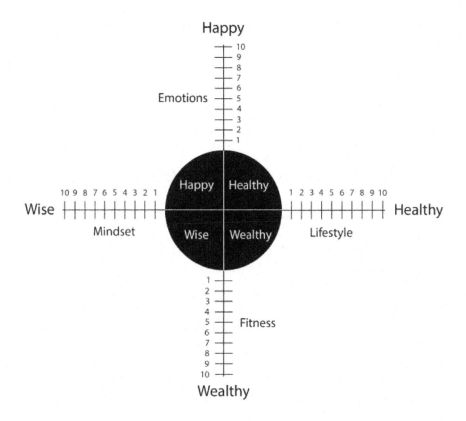

"Increasing your self-esteem is easy.
Simply do good things and
remember that you did them."

John-Roger

Chapter 6: Take Charge – Diagnose

After the soul searching sessions in 'Part 1 – Take Stock', it's time to progress and Take Charge. As part of your Suddenly Single Journey, you should have a much better understanding of your emotions and where you are on the Change Curve. You should understand your 'Why' and have reflected on your accomplishments, disappointments and learning from the past 12 months. You understand your personal values, have set goals and worked on your bucket list. You should have a more positive attitude towards your future, have started to get your monkeys under control and feel part of the Suddenly Single Community, sharing Little Wins and Friday Toasts.

Well done! You are making progress.

Now it's time to find out...

The truth about money

- How much money is enough?
- How much do you need to earn?
- How much do you need to save?
- Will you run out of money?
- What do you need to do to ensure your family has complete peace of mind?

Mary had asked herself these very questions

"I'd never really had much to do with money. Richard had always sorted all those things, paid the bills, and organised our savings and

pensions. Here I was without a clue of what we had or where it was. But I knew I needed to learn quickly. Could I still maintain my lifestyle, and have the life I wanted?"

The Suddenly Single process will help you review the key considerations so you can answer all these questions.

1. Where are you now?

A detailed income and expenditure sheet is a must. People always underestimate what they spend. It is important to have a comprehensive assessment of monthly income and expenditure. A good discipline to ensure it is accurate is to log daily spending over a three-month period and input the data.

	MONTHLY SPEND	DESIRED SPEND
Home		
Insurance		
Eats, Drinks & Smokes		
Transport & Travel		
Debt Repayments		
Savings & Investments		
Family		
Funs & Frolics		
Health & Beauty		
Clothes		
Education & Courses		
Big One-Offs		
Odds & Sods		

Practical Tip

Go to www.suddenly-single.co.uk and complete the detailed expenditure spreadsheet.

2. How much have I got and where is it?

Often, during a probate or divorce process, you will be provided with a detailed analysis of all assets and liabilities. Collect all of this data and put this in to your personal balance sheet.

ASSETS	LAST YEAR	THIS YEAR
Home & Contents		
Bank Accounts		
Investments (shares, bonds, ISAs etc.)		
Pensions		
Car		
Jewellery		
Loans to family/ friends/inheritances		
Other		
TOTAL		

LIABILITIES	LAST YEAR	THIS YEAR
Mortgage		
Car Loan		
Personal Loan		
Credit Card		
Loans from family/ friends		
Other		
TOTAL		

"Assets put money in your pocket,

whether you work or not,

and liabilities take money from your pocket."

Robert Kiyosaki

3. What do I need to change?

Create a priority to-do list. Write down everything that is/was in joint names or your partner's name that now needs switching to a single name. Don't forget that social media and professional sites such as LinkedIn and Google searches can assist with this.

4. Staying safe, not making the situation worse

Have you updated your will and considered lasting powers of attorney? Are you paying the correct amount of tax? Many people don't consider these subjects until it is too late, which is likely to mean you pay more tax than you need to and the wrong people benefit from all your hard work in building your assets.

Gwen reflected on point 4...

"I had only just finished dealing with probate following my father's death, then Roy had passed away without updating our wills or having a lasting power of attorney. I knew I needed help to sort everything out. This was all well and good but who could help me with these things? Luckily for me, Roy had engaged with a specialist before he passed away and Jo Read had helped him organise his finances. But who should you trust? How do you pick the right professionals to help?"

5. Who should I trust?

Engage with the right professional team.

I have created a list of the things that most Suddenly Singles want when they are selecting their professional team:

- Peace of mind and freedom from worry
- Personalised communications that are relevant to them
- Responsiveness and accessibility, knowing they are at the end of a phone if help is needed
- Speak using simple terms that you can easily understand
- Put things right when they go wrong
- To be treated as an individual and with empathy
- Deliver what they promise
- Not given reams of paperwork, generic information and irrelevant communications
- Not to be sold to
- Not to have meetings that resemble endurance tests

Having the right professionals for the job is essential and will save you time and money in the long run. But who is the right team and how do you pick them?

- **The Lawyer** – You need to hire a lawyer experienced in family law, who can help you through all legal aspects of divorce or bereavement. They don't need to be expensive; they just need to possess the three key attributes, experienced, qualified and integrous. They should speak in plain English. They should be someone you trust and feel comfortable with because you may have to reveal highly personal information about yourself and your marriage and life. Where possible, seek a testimonial.
  http://solicitors.lawsociety.org.uk/

- **The Financial Adviser** – A good financial adviser is integral to a Happy, Healthy, Wealthy and Wise woman. A good financial adviser takes time to understand you, your goals and objectives, and what your fears and worries are. They should be someone who takes time to explain things so you understand. They will build a roadmap of your future and support you along the journey, helping you save time, money and tax. They will help you avoid making all the common mistakes and show you how to map your money to your goals. They liaise with all of your professional adviser team and act as the glue to achieving your objectives.

- **The Accountant** – There are many types of tax and tax allowances. Using a qualified accountant helps you work through the tax maze and will save you money and time. Look for someone who can act as a business partner. The right accountant will have more than just prestige – it's important they understand your needs, and are able to offer relevant insight.

  http://www.icaew.com/en/about-icaew/find-a-chartered-accountant

Visit www.suddenly-single.co.uk for professionals that we have worked with and have been recommended to the Suddenly Single Community.

Practical Tips from Gwen's experience

1. Get copies of your financial paperwork, understand what needs to be paid and when. Make sure you can access any joint bank accounts. Make sure you have a bank account open already in your name with an emergency fund.

2. Operate two separate filing systems. One contains current year paper copies of all financial paperwork, under the headings;

    HOUSE; BANK; BILLS; CREDIT CARDS; EMPLOYMENT; SAVINGS; PERSONAL; CAR.

    I operate a cloud-based long-term storage system where I scan and save each year's documents. I use Dropbox as I find it simple to use. Alternatively paper copies can be kept in a water and fire resistant safe.

3. Complete the three-month budget planner analysis.

4. Sign up to money saving sites such as www.moneysavingexpert.com

5. Ask your friends and network for recommendations for the professionals listed above.

6. Update your will and make sure you fully understand it too. Almost two-thirds of us will die intestate; that is without a valid will. It is a common misconception that dying intestate results in "what I would do anyway". Homemade wills can be a problem too; though made with the best of intentions, they are usually unsatisfactory and often invalid.

There are strict rules relating to signing wills and one mistake in this process will render it invalid. Tax planning opportunities are often ignored too.

Practical Tips from Mary's experience

1. If you are getting divorced, break all financial ties, and set up your own bank account and direct debits (most banks can do this). Take care not to miss payments. This can damage your credit score.

2. Understand the marital assets, in particular pensions and investments. The terminology can often be confusing;

   • Offsetting
   • Earmarking
   • Pension sharing

   Early advice is invaluable. In a divorce settlement, the priority is finding the pension assets and ensuring they are properly valued.

   There are many types of pensions. Financial advisers and lawyers are well placed to quickly identify if a pension value looks too low. They will also assist you in identifying financial assets and help ensure that full disclosure has taken place.

3. Don't get emotionally attached to certain assets. I loved my house; I didn't see it as an asset; it was where I found sanctuary, entertained and relaxed. But I couldn't really afford it and had to educate myself that it wasn't integral to my happiness.

4. Remember that all debt isn't bad, I wish I'd made different decisions around having a mortgage. I took the home mortgage free, but did not have sufficient income to achieve my goals. I'd come from a generation that spent their whole life paying off mortgages and therefore had a real reticence about borrowing again. I discovered debt isn't necessarily a demon, particularly with low interest rates; it just needs to be respected, understood and become part of your overall personal business plan.

5. Take advice as early as possible. My financial adviser was able to increase my overall financial settlement through his detailed analysis of all of our investments and pensions. I had never completed any type of cash flow forecasting and had no idea what it was, but with guidance, I was able to do this (this is really just thinking ahead about what money is coming in and going out and writing it down, so you can see how it balances out). The cash flow forecast helped me visualise my goals, bring them to life and show me how I could fund them.

6. Make a lasting power of attorney. I found this fact sheet very helpful in helping me understand what one was and why I needed it.

What are lasting powers of attorney?

Lasting powers of attorney (LPAs) are legal documents that enable you to name a person or persons (your attorney/s) to take decisions on your behalf in the event that you become incapable of making decisions yourself. There are two types of LPA: an LPA for property and financial affairs, and an LPA for health and welfare. The former allows your attorneys to take decisions on your behalf regarding your assets and finances, including matters such as buying and selling properties, managing your investments, paying your expenses and completing your tax return. The latter gives your attorneys authority to take welfare and healthcare decisions on your behalf, such as where and with whom you live, what you wear and how you spend your day and also to give and refuse consent to medical treatment, including life sustaining treatment if you wish.

Making a lasting power of attorney avoids your family having to go down the route of the Court of Protection and allows you to appoint people you trust to make decisions regarding health and welfare as well as property and finances. Should you suffer any mental incapacity or become unable to cope with making your own financial decisions, at the very least you will have the peace of mind that your loved ones have the authority to make sure your wishes are carried out.

Why do you need a lasting power of attorney?

1. You choose the people who you want to look after your financial and personal welfare affairs in the event of deterioration in mental capacity.

2. It avoids the need for loved ones to make an application to the Court of Protection which can be time-consuming and costly. The delays can have a big impact on you financially as your assets are electively frozen.

3. For peace of mind, your everyday financial transactions will continue to be dealt with such as paying bills and operating a bank account, and receiving your benefits, pensions and allowances. Your wishes will be carried out on matters, such as medical treatment, day-to-day issues and living arrangements.

"Keep your dreams alive.
Understand to achieve anything
requires faith and belief in yourself,
vision, hard work, determination,
and dedication.
Remember all things are possible
for those who believe."

Gail Devers

Chapter 7: Take Charge – Take Action

So how are you feeling?

You should feel more in control and more confident about what you want and what you have got. You have picked the right team and its time to get down to the nitty-gritty.

Let's get SMART with your money. This chapter will explore how to make your money go further and how to make the right financial choices.

Being in control of your money for the first time can be daunting. These are some of the questions I often get asked by Suddenly Singles:

- Will I have enough money in the future to do what I want?
- Can I make any further reductions in my monthly spending?
- Am I saving and investing in the right place?
- Am I paying too much tax?
- How can I keep an eye on my investments?
- How can I make sure my children don't pay too much tax when I die?

To help you answer the questions above, I ask Suddenly Singles to complete the following actions:

1. Hunt through all of your paperwork and complete a detailed summary of your assets and liabilities. It's really important to understand in detail where your money is invested and if it is still meeting expectations. Plans and products improve over time so it's worth fully understanding the options.

2. List down all the policies and plans that you have in an authority letter, including the company name and policy number. This enables your adviser to write to all of the companies and ask a detailed list of questions that ensures you get all the relevant facts about what you have.

3. Assess how and where you spend your money. Complete a spending diary for one month using the expenditure spreadsheet. Write down everything you spend from coffees to lunches, birthdays and holidays.

4. Review the 'How to save money tip sheet' and '10 Steps to a Wealthier Retirement' information sheets. This will help build your knowledge in these areas. Don't worry; you don't need to become an expert, just get familiar with your options. Have a look at these information sheets on www.suddenly-single.co.uk

5. Map your income to your outgoings. In an ideal world, the numbers should look like this:

- 50% of your income should be spent on essential needs.
- 20% should be saved for rainy day money/short-term and long-term projects.
- 30% should be on discretionary spend, things you want but do not need.

Budgeting can be tough if you have never done it. I like to split budgets into three components:

Your Basic Budget:

This is your lowest possible budget and your essential spending. It will pay your food and housing costs, but little more.

Eliminating debt is very important as interest will need to be paid, so understanding your liabilities is also important. Paying off any debts can eliminate interest payments from your budget.

Your Lifestyle Budget:

This budget meets your current and expected living expenses, plus your lifestyle expenses i.e. discretionary spend, such as entertainment and holidays.

Your Aspirational Budget:

This budget includes your dreams, even those that may be impossible to meet! It allows you to highlight some of the events or activities you would like to be able to experience. It can also include the things that you definitely want to do, like celebrate a big anniversary in style, pay for a grandchild's wedding, or go on a special trip abroad... These are items that are out of your normal expenditure but that you would like to be able to fund from your income, before and during retirement.

This can include items on your bucket list!

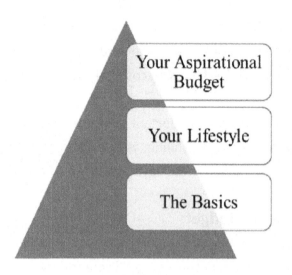

Gwen reflected on what she had learnt so far:

"I was really concerned with understanding my assets; I had inherited a plethora of different plans from both my father and husband. I had bonds, shares, ISAs, numerous savings accounts, pensions and many more... It was a maze of paper. Should I keep the mortgage? Which savings account was best? Should I stay in the property? Should I sell the shares? I didn't know where to start. With Jo's help and some of the habits I had adopted from Stephen Covey's book, 'The 7 Habits of Highly Effective People', I was able to make inroads into this maze.

"Habit 2 – Begin with the end in mind...

"What was important to me? What did I want to get done in my life?

"I was very keen to pay as little tax as possible. Both Roy and my father had been avid investors and I thought they would turn in their graves if I didn't continue investing with a plan to pay as little tax as possible! Again, with assistance from Jo, my accountant and lawyer, I began

to understand all the different taxes; Income Tax, Capital Gains Tax, Inheritance Tax and all the products that are tax advantaged, such as pensions and ISAs."

Mary was more concerned with when she could retire. She read with interest the '10 Steps to a Wealthier Retirement' fact sheet.

1. Find out all about your state pension and how to increase it
2. Track down old pensions and investments
3. Are your pensions working hard enough for you?
4. Survive and thrive in the annuity jungle
5. Pay the right tax
6. Downsize and equity release
7. Understand purchased life annuity and income drawdown
8. Long-term care and asset protection trusts
9. Understand Inheritance Tax
10. Make a will and lasting power of attorney

"There seemed a lot of jargon in this fact sheet but Jo took the time to cover each one so I understood all of my options. We set to work on each point. It is great to work with someone who can give you peace of mind and clarity over something that I had always found boring and complex."

Let's pause for a breath...

So what do you now know?

1. What money and debt you have and where it is
2. How much you have coming in and going out
3. What your basic, lifestyle and aspirational budgets should look like
4. Tips on saving money
5. How to retire with as much money as possible

Practical Tip

Read the fact sheets listed in this chapter.

Don't freak out, money doesn't have to be complicated but it is time now if you haven't already to engage with a financial adviser.

Now we know what we have, it's time to map the numbers to your goals and objectives. This is where it gets a bit technical and your professional team needs to work together to get this right, but in essence they consider a five-pot strategy.

1. Cash management – rainy day money, picking the best accounts
2. Investing in plans that use all your income tax allowances and may reduce income tax, now and in retirement
3. Investing in plans that use all your capital gains tax allowances
4. Investing in plans that use all of your inheritance tax allowances
5. The best of the rest – when the above pots are filled, how to structure remaining assets

Visit www.suddenly-single.co.uk for more information

Gwen now felt more confident around her money and plans, and reviewed the original questions that had concerned her

- **Will I have enough money in the future to do what I want?**

  "Pensions had always been a mystery to me and I felt they needed to be in one place so I could easily understand and monitor them. I had accumulated company and personal pensions and inherited another two pots from Roy. I never really understood what I was going to retire on. As part of understanding my assets, Jo tidied up my pensions, helped me sort out the pensions I had inherited from Roy, and completed a forecast. I now have peace of mind that I won't run out of money in retirement."

- **Can I make any further reductions in my monthly spending?**

  "I had read with interest the tips on how to save money and knew that Roy would have been proud of my new-found financial acumen. I made significant savings by following the tips on utilities, mobile phones, broadband and insurance. I now feel in control of my budgets and spending."

- **Am I saving and investing in the right place? How can I keep an eye on my investments?**

  "This was probably the biggest learning curve that I went through. I didn't have a clue and the terminology was very new to me: diversification, risk, asset classes and allocation. Jo took time to help me understand what level of risk I was comfortable with and what I wanted my money to do. A portfolio was constructed that matched my attitude to risk, objectives and expectations, and I receive regular reports that help me check my progress. I know I've picked a trusted adviser to select, monitor and review my investments to help me achieve financial independence."

- **Am I paying too much tax and how can I make sure my children don't pay too much inheritance tax?**

 "I now have a five-pot strategy that enables me to maximise the use of all my tax allowances. These are reviewed regularly and updated when the Chancellor makes changes in his budgets. I have managed to reduce my inheritance tax liability by 25% and will be making further reductions over the next few years through regular planning. I now believe Inheritance Tax is a voluntary tax, and through careful planning I hope to reduce this significantly."

A good financial adviser helps you save:

TIME, MONEY AND TAX...

This is true, but I believe it is so much more than that. Good financial planning helps bring your dreams to life. Let's face it, money just gets stuff done!

Mary echoed these sentiments. What she had found particularly useful In the Take Charge stage was the report that she received.

It was called a cash flow forecast plan.

A cash flow forecast is a really good tool and report that helps you clearly visualise milestones in your life such as big holidays, children's weddings, retiring, and more. If you are a visual person, this report will help bring your goals and dreams to life. It maps your assets and income to your milestones, and shows you what you can afford and for how long. Completing a cash flow forecast can be a useful exercise in answering these questions:

How long will my money last?

Can I afford to maintain my lifestyle?

Suddenly Singles get particularly excited about allocating their 'Wild Living Money', a phrase I use to help put some fun in to money and help visualise the future.

Mary shared the report she had been given.

It had given her peace of mind and the confidence to pursue her dreams.

Summary Report

Following on from our cash flow plan meeting, I have updated the details to represent the events, costs and changes we discussed. This report should help give you clarity over your financial future and peace of mind in knowing you can continue to live a good life.

Summary of additions/changes

- *Your mortgage has now been repaid and the data updated in your cash flow projections.*

- *Holidays and capital outlay planned:*
  - *Costa Rica – next year @ £5,000*
  - *Annual budget – increased to £6,000 to allow for you to complete some of your bucket list*

- *Wild Living – an ad hoc annual cost of £3,000 has been entered (for emergency costs/holidays/entertaining)*

- *Grandchildren's wedding costs – £20,000 added in for years in the future*

- *Fully retiring at age 60*

Retirement

We discussed stopping full-time work at 60. This would reduce your income and pension so it was important to understand the potential impact of this. For this plan, I have assumed you retire at 60 and do not continue working as this would have the most impact on your income and assets.

Later life

We touch on your later life. You identified that at roughly age 80, you would want to move into a care home rather than risk becoming a burden on your children. I have assumed that you sell your new flat at age 80 to release the capital, then reduce some of your lifestyle expenses and pay an additional £45,000 p.a. in care home fees.

Plan results – is it achievable?

Yes.

Based on your current assets and our economic assumptions, the above changes should be affordable. You shouldn't run out of capital and could, if you decided to, gift further capital in the future.

If you decide to work part-time from 60, rather than stopping completely, this will only have a positive effect on your future income and capital. However, you should have the ability to stop working completely at age 60.

"The hardest thing in the world to understand is the Income Tax."

Albert Einstein

Chapter 8: Take Charge – In Control

You should now be feeling more in control and see a future with happiness, where you don't have to worry about money and you are excited about the goals you have set and can achieve.

So what have you learned so far on your Suddenly Single Journey?

TAKE STOCK

1. Internalise – you now understand the Journey of Change and the stages that you go through. You should be nearing acceptance but remember there will be times when you drift back. This is normal; just use the Suddenly Single Community for support. You understand 'Why' you are who you are. You have focused on the 10 questions and are firmly in charge of having 'Your Best Year Yet'!

2. Envision – you have a much clearer picture on where you want to be. You have considered your personal values and set your personal goals. You've reviewed the habits that create effective people. You've had some fun creating your bucket list!

3. Negative to Positive – you have taken time to forgive, forget and learn. Your 'monkeys' are firmly under control. You are having fun sharing your 'Little Wins' and 'Friday Toasts' with your support network and the Suddenly Single Community.

TAKE CHARGE

4. Diagnose – you understand the truth about money: you know what you have and where it is. You know what you need to change and the importance of wills and lasting powers of attorney. But more importantly, you have chosen a team of trusted advisers.

5. Take Action – you understand how to be smart with money. You can manage your basic, lifestyle and aspirational budgets. You have increased your knowledge around retirement and tax, and know how to spend your wild living money!

This is great and you are making real progress. But there's still more to do and learn on our Suddenly Single Journey, and our quest to become happier, healthier, wealthier and wise.

Remember, lifestyle financial planning is an ONGOING process; it requires regular maintenance. Just like getting fit, you can't go to the gym once and expect to be fit for life. In order to stay in control, you must review your situation on a regular basis.

Let's look at some more ideas to help you take charge and control. Once you know what you have, where it is and what you want, it's important to document all of this in a safe place. A place you can easily find and share when necessary. If you have ever tried to sort out someone's affairs when they have passed away, you know that this can be a minefield. There are papers and documents everywhere, often going back years.

So wouldn't it be great to have everything you need in one document? This would be a divorce lawyer or executor's dream. So let's do it, let's create a place to record everything from bank accounts to music requests when you pass away.

My Suddenly Single Documents

My Suddenly Single Documents forms the basis of Staying In Control. It is a document that lists what you own and where it is kept. It contains all information pertinent to your life, things like your will, shares certificates, bank account details, life assurance plans and much more, all of which would need to be accessed shortly after death, loss of capacity or divorce. People often struggle to collate this information but when you've been through the pain of doing it once, it's very easy to keep updated.

The death of a close family member or friend is always a traumatic time for those left behind. It is often made more difficult for those relatives or friends who have been asked to be executors and to deal with the probate because they often have difficulty in finding key documents and other important information that belonged to the deceased.

Important things as listed above all need to be accessible shortly after death and for probate.

The term 'probate' means the entire process of estate administration after death: obtaining details of what the individual has left, going through the process of gaining authority to deal with the deceased's estate, paying off any debts or clearing liabilities including any Inheritance Tax, and finally distributing any remaining assets to those entitled to receive them. Probate is only granted where the deceased left a will. The grant of probate of the will is a court order that gives the executors of the will the right to deal with the assets and property of the person who has died. For example, when you show the grant of probate to a bank, they know they are dealing with the person who is allowed to handle the estate and they will allow you to close the deceased's account.

There are different processes depending on the type of 'grant' being applied for.

- Grant of probate
  Where the deceased left a will that appointed one or more personal representatives, called 'executors', and a minimum of one is willing to act.

- Letters of administration with will annexed
  Where the deceased left a will but did not appoint personal representatives or those appointed died before the deceased or are unwilling or unable to act.

- Letters of administration
  Where the deceased died without a will, referred to as dying 'intestate' (including where the will is invalid).

'The probate process' can be found at www.suddenly-single.co.uk

Quite apart from making the job harder for the executors, it is possible that some assets may go undetected. For example, you may have a paid-up life insurance plan – in other words, a plan where there are no more premiums payable, but which still provides benefits. If the plan documentation has been lost, or is hidden away somewhere, how will the executors know? Their families have no knowledge of the plan and so the money will be lost to them. The position is similar with UK banks. There are vast sums of unclaimed monies held by National Savings & Investments. Although the banks and other financial institutions do their utmost to trace account holders and repay this, a significant amount of client funds lie unclaimed.

Clearly, you can make it much easier if your affairs are in good order and your family or friends don't have to search high and low for documents that they don't even know exist.

It also means that the heirs will receive the full inheritance that you intended for them to receive more quickly than if someone has to search for assets.

My Documents Checklist, which follows on the next few pages,
can also be found on www.suddenly-single.co.uk

This will enable you to keep track of all your assets and, in particular, to let your family know their physical location.

It also includes a Key Contacts Checklist, which enables you to list the details of your important advisers, such as your solicitor, accountant and financial adviser. Once you have completed the checklist, take a copy for key members of your family.

Practical Tip

Take time to work through and complete the document checklist and your letter of wishes.

My Documents Checklist –
What I Own and Where it is Kept

Name:	
National Insurance Number:	
Tax Reference:	
Date of Birth:	

My Will:

NAME AND ADDRESS	CONTACT
Financial Adviser:	
Solicitor:	
Accountant:	
Doctor:	
Tax Office:	
Employer:	
Others:	

My Will:

The original of my will is held with:	
The will is dated:	
The will was drawn up by:	
My executors are:	

Claiming the Transferable Nil Rate Band:

When an individual dies who was previously married or in a civil partnership, a claim can be made to transfer the nil rate band, where any part of it was unused, from the spouse or civil partner who died first. The following documents will be needed in support of such a claim. Please use this section to record their location.

Copy of Grant of Representation (Confirmation in Scotland) of deceased spouse/civil partner:	
Will of deceased spouse/civil partner:	
Any Deed of Variation or disclaimer executed in respect of property inherited from a deceased spouse/civil partner:	
Death certificate of deceased spouse/civil partner:	

My Attorneys:

Date made	Name and address of Attorneys	Has it been registered? YES/NO	Names and addresses of individuals to be notified of any application to register the EPA/LPA

Bank/Building Society Accounts (including online accounts):

Bank/Building Society (Name and Address of Branch)	Sort Code	Account No	Contact

Credit Cards (including online accounts):

Credit Card Company	Account No	Contact

Loans:

Company	Account No	Contact

My Assets:

Investment Bonds/Unit Trust	Investment Detail	Plan No/ Account No	Contact

PEP/ISAs	Investment Detail	Plan No/ Account No	Contact

Savings & Life Assurance Plans	Investment Detail	Plan No/ Account No	Contact

Stocks & Shares	Investment Detail	Plan No/ Account No	Contact

Other Assets	Investment Detail	Plan No/ Account No	Contact

Comments/Notes

My Pension:

Provider (Name and Address)	Latest Plan Value	Plan Number	Contact

My Property:

Type	Address	Approximate Value	Ownership	Loan
Main Residence				
Other Property				

Comments/Notes

Gifts made during lifetime:

Date	Amount and/or Asset	Recipient of Gift

Surplus Income:

Income

Tax Year In Which Gifts Made					
Salary					
Pensions					
Interest					
Investments					
Rents					
Annuities (income element)					
Other					
Minus Income Tax Paid					
Net Income					

Surplus Income:

Expenditure

Mortgages					
Insurance					
Household Bills					
Council Tax					
Travelling Costs					
Entertainment					
Holidays					
Nursing Home Fees					
Other					
Total Expenditure					
Surplus Income					
Gifts Made					

Miscellaneous Information:

Details of Organisations and Clubs:

Name	Membership	Contact

Other Contacts (Utility Companies, General Insurance, Magazines):

Name	Account/Member	Contact

Additional Information e.g. where information is stored

Funeral Arrangements

The death of someone special can be a time of great stress as well as distress for the bereaved. We can lessen that stress for those we leave behind by making our wishes for our funeral known beforehand. With this in mind, the following chart may be of help.

Remember, you do not have to complete all or indeed any of the questions asked. But the more you do answer, the greater the help you will be offering your next of kin.

Cremation: Yes ☐   No ☐
If yes:
Ashes Interred?   Yes ☐   No ☐
Ashes Scattered?   Yes ☐   No ☐
Burial?   Yes ☐   No ☐

If yes, where? (Legal restrictions will apply)

....

....

Service in church: Yes ☐   No ☐
If yes, which church?

....

The service

Music at entry? ....

Hymns to sing?   Yes □   No □

If yes, list up to three:

1. ....

2. ....

3. ....

Reading? ....

Any special tribute and if so, by whom?..............................

Music at exit?...

Any other wishes?..

....

....

....

Electronic data/information/passwords

Please use this section to record either details of the whereabouts of any data that may be stored electronically, such as online accounts, including security information and passwords, plus any requests in respect of data or information to be deleted or passed on.

Other Information:

Please use this section to record any additional information e.g. requests regarding medical research bequests, deed/safe box access etc.

You have now completed the second module of the Suddenly Single Journey, Take Charge.

Let's see what progress you have made on the HHWW scale.

HAPPY – You've completed your aspirational budgets and now have a cash flow forecast which maps your dreams and goals with your money. You know what wild living money you have available!

HEALTHY – You've evaluated your health and lifestyle and set goals. You now know what these cost and what options are most suitable for your budget.

WEALTHY – You've dealt with the nitty-gritty of money. You know what you have got, where it is and you've taken steps to stay safe, by making wills and lasting powers of attorney. You have completed 'My Suddenly Single Documents' and have a plan for the future.

WISE – You know how to find the right advisers and who to trust. You have become smart with your money and know how to save time, money and tax. You know the right questions to ask yourself to have 'Your Best Year Yet', you understand your 'Why' and the habits of effective people. You understand your monkeys and how to tame them!

Why don't you take time to score yourself?

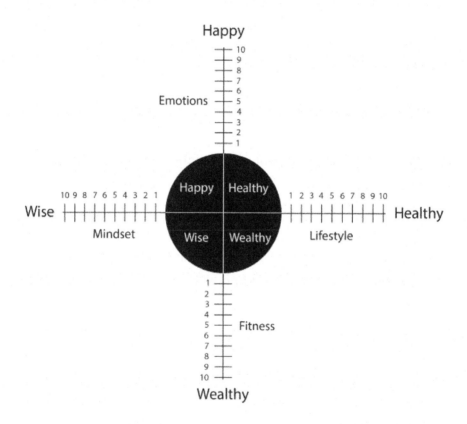

Chapter 9: Take Off – Troubleshoot

We constantly experience change and it is therefore important that we take time to review the plans we have put in place to help us achieve our goals.

The planning strategies we have put in place may need to be changed and therefore constant monitoring is a necessity. It is important to stay in touch with the triggers that prompt the need to change; this is particularly relevant in the world of finance. Constant legislation, product, economic and global changes make it imperative to have a communication channel with your advisers to ensure changes are implemented quickly.

As part of the Suddenly Single Journey, we always conduct annual troubleshooting meetings. These are a vital part of the Take Off module. It is important to meet with all your advisers on a regular basis to see if anything needs to be changed. During these meetings, we re-evaluate all of the elements of the Suddenly Single Journey, to ensure everything is still on track.

Let's review Mary's last troubleshooting meeting.

Mary had been inspired throughout her Suddenly Single modules and now looked forward to her review meetings. She explains why...

"When I first started on my Suddenly Single Journey, I had been very quiet and withdrawn, my moods were dark and I thought I would never see the light at the end of the tunnel. But now I embrace change. I have taken control back and actively encourage those in the Suddenly

Single Community to do the same. I love my annual review meetings as they are evidence to me of how far I have come. I love the do, plan, review feeling that I have after following the process.

"Here is a summary of my last review meeting;

1. **Where are you on the Journey of Change? Do any issues need attention?**

   "I can say with conviction that I have reached Stage 6 – I feel fully empowered, secure, and my self-esteem has returned. My life now has meaning and I am confident that I have a bright future. I can see the light and it's very bright!"

2. **Where are you now financially?**

   "I regularly review my budget planners and my desired outgoings against actual outgoings. I have become very disciplined at keeping these records. I did, however, feel out of kilter on a couple of expenses. I was spending too much on beauty and health and felt my utilities and insurances were too high. I visited www. moneysavingexpert.com for some guidance. By following some of the tips, I've made changes to my utilities and insurance providers and was pleased to have saved several hundred pounds. I also signed up to some discount sites such as Groupon and Living Social so I could purchase discounted beauty treatments."

3. **Do you know how much you have got and where it is?**

   "Jo, my financial adviser, regularly provides me with up-to-date valuations of all my assets and liabilities. I can then update my personal balance sheet. At this review, I was pleased to see that all of my investments had gone up in value."

4. **Are your wills, trusts and lasting powers of attorney accurate and up to date?**

"I now have a six-month-old grandchild and was keen to make some provision for her in my will, so I met with my lawyer to update my will. Sadly my brother also passed away earlier in the year and he had been my executor and trustee, so at the same meeting I was able to organise the paperwork to remove and replace him."

5. **Are you achieving your goals and working through your bucket list?**

"I had set three goals at the start of the year, to recognise my Little Wins daily, lose weight through exercise and complete a social media course. I was on track with all three. I had lost two stone after following 'Fun & Fit programme' recommended by my personal trainer. I knew that I had to stay focused, however as I had also been active on my bucket list, which involved visiting three Michelin star restaurants this year, not a good combination with my fitness goals!"

6. **Review cash flow forecast – Are you still on track?**

"I had watched with interest as Jo, my financial adviser, updated the valuations and added events to my timeline. The forecast didn't look quite as good as it had previously and the red section as explained represented a shortfall in income and capital. I had been overspending and this was evident with the block of red!

"I wanted to understand my options. I had already taken steps to reduce some of my spending. We now had to consider other options; Jo suggested we look at my investment strategy. By changing this, I could potentially achieve more growth on my investments. This had the desired effect when the new numbers

were added to the cash flow of removing the red. I had always considered myself a risk-taker and I was keen to continue to spend my 'Wild Living money'. I had a good income and cash behind me and felt comfortable with a change to my investment strategy."

7. Is there anything worrying you? Do you need to calm the monkeys?

"Learning to manage my monkey mind had been a real challenge. I had further disappointments this year with the death of my brother and the monkeys had once again returned.

"'Why me again? Everyone I love seems to be taken' I now understood what was going on in my head and chatted calmly back. I still have lots of people in my life that I love and I continue to make strong friendships. I am loved back by many. I refocused on my Little Wins and this also helped to tame the monkeys. Exercise and meditation had become an activity I regularly followed; these too helped to tame the monkeys!"

8. How is the five-pot strategy looking?

"My financial adviser, Jo, regularly updated me on legislation, product and relevant tax changes. I preferred this by brief emails and then a more detailed discussion at my review meeting. This ensured I was still taking full advantage of the changes and had the right plans in place. I always had a meeting before the end of the tax year to ensure I had made the most of all my tax allowances.

"Jo provided me with a personal tax checklist. In advance of the end of the tax year on 5 April, there are always a number of planning points that you may wish to consider.

"Jo explained the main points that she would consider on my behalf;

- *Minimising your exposure to higher rates of income tax*
- *Reviewing your investments to ensure tax efficiency*
- *Protecting your wealth and minimising Inheritance Tax*
- *Retirement planning, utilising and reviewing all allowances*
- *Maximising Capital Gains Tax Allowance."*

9. Do you need to make updates to 'My Suddenly Single Documents'?

"I now kept this document with my Will and lasting power of attorney. Having recently dealt with a probate, I knew only too well the perils and time that it took to locate assets and liaise with solicitors and insurance companies."

10. Are you happy with your advisers and are they adding value?

"I had been heavily dependent on my advisers over the past 12 months and I am convinced that having the right professionals for the job is essential. I was pleasantly surprised when Jo went through a value added checklist, which clearly demonstrated the time, money and tax I had saved by working with my team.

"I now know so much more. I don't need to know all the jargon, just the simple truth about money; money gets things done and lets me live the life I want. When you pick an adviser you can trust, you need to consider the following:

- *Do you feel at ease with them?*
- *Do they understand your situation?*

- *Do they inspire you and give you confidence?*
- *Do they explain things in a language you understand?*
- *Do they specialise in a particular area and have the appropriate qualifications?*

"I can answer yes to all these questions and here's the evidence; she handed a copy of her value added checklist to me at our last meeting."

Are you getting Added Value from your adviser?

Value Added Checklist

Client Name	Mary
Value Added Area	Benefit to client (In £ where possible)

Investment

	Investments have increased in value by 6%, £66,000. Pension consolidation saved £1,500 in fees per annum. Active cash management increased cash interest by £800p.a.
• Extra returns • Costs saved	

Tax

• Pension Tax savings • CGT Tax savings • Investment Earnings Tax savings • Income Tax savings • PAYE/NI savings	• Pension contribution generated £5,000 Income Tax Relief. • Restructure of share portfolio utilised £11,000 Capital Gains Tax Allowance. • Fully-funded ISAs

Insurance

• Premiums paid • Claims paid out • Quality of cover (definitions) increased • Insurance Premium Savings	Restructured Inheritance Tax insurance policy and saved £1,200p.a.

Education

• Books recommended to client • Articles provided to client • Seminars held for client • External seminars recommended to client	• *Start with Why* by Simon Sinek • *Your Best Year Yet* by Jinny Ditzler • *The 7 Habits of Highly Effective People* by Stephen Covey • 'Suddenly Single' Seminar attended

Debt

• Interest saved • Debt made tax deductible & tax saved • Debt eliminated • Debt created (& value added as a result) • Debt re-structured successfully	Repaid mortgage

Estate planning

• Wills established • Trusts established (& assets or people protected as a result) • IHT saved • Other tax saved	• Deed of variation on brother's estate. • Wills and lasting powers of attorney established • Inheritance Tax planning through trusts, Inheritance Tax saving £212,000

Problems avoided

• Recommendations to NOT do something • Strategies or structures established that avoid problems in the future	Full Inheritance Tax mitigation strategy in place

Other Professionals

• Referrals to other professionals • Tax saved as a result • Costs avoided as a result • Structures established as a result • Any benefits from advice given	• Referral to will writing service • Referral to a personal trainer; lost two stone

Administration hassle

• Stuff-ups fixed without the clients knowledge • Stuff-ups fixed raised by the client (hours spent) • Benefits of fixing the stuff-ups	• Help in Tax Return completion avoided HMRC fine • Liaised with Deed of Variation lawyer to remove £125,000 from estate with no tax

"I know it looks complicated but having a team of advisers that you trust and who understand you gives you all the confidence you need.

"Yes, you need to find a home for the money, and yes you need to keep an eye on it, even shift it around occasionally.

"Yes, you need to decide on a solid investment philosophy.

"Yes, you need to tweak with things to make stuff tax-efficient and use up various tax allowances. But as my financial adviser explained, lifestyle planning is not about products, investment philosophy and tax. These are just tools to help you achieve your goals, and for me these are being Happy Healthy, Wealthy and Wise."

"Independence is a heady draught,
and if you drink it in your youth,
it can have the same effect on the brain
as young wine does.
It does not matter that its taste
is not always appealing.
It is addictive and with each drink
you want more."

Maya Angelou

Chapter 10: Take Off – Yes, you've made it!

Congratulations, your world has changed and so have you!

You've completed the Suddenly Single Journey.

Take Stock, Take Charge and Take Off

You should now feel more confident around money and what this means to your future. You're empowered to control and influence your own happiness, health, wealth and wisdom. The monkeys are under control, and you have a better relationship with money and what lies ahead.

Let's just recap on what you have achieved:

- You have reached acceptance on the Journey of Change
- You have experienced 'Your Best Year Yet'
- You now have peace of mind, are better organised financially and free from financial worries
- You have the right professionals aligned to your goals
- You have a list of goals linked to your values
- You are having fun with your bucket list
- The monkeys are under control
- You understand the truth about money and strive to achieve the 50/20/30 principles (see pages 81-83 for budgeting advice)
- You are being smart with your money and following the five-pot strategy to a wealthier retirement
- You know what you have got and where it is kept, and this is documented in 'My Suddenly Single Documents'

- You hold annual meetings with your advisers to ensure you are on track.

Mary shared how she felt at this point;

"The Suddenly Single Journey has transformed how I feel and all that is important to me. I've replaced my anger with assertiveness. I'm now able to articulate what I think, feel and want in my life. I've accepted that change is inevitable, my focus is firmly on the future I have and I'm proud of the progress I have made. The feelings I now experience are acceptance, hope and trust. Occasionally I drift back but with regular communication and support from the Suddenly Single Community and my friends, I stay on track.

"This journey has helped me to get more out of life by creating a sense of urgency; get things done; live life to the full; do stuff now, before it's too late. Life is not a rehearsal.

"I now allow myself to think about new possibilities and feel enthusiastic about my future. I believe that you are in control of your happiness – circumstances don't create our happiness and contentment, that's our job."

Gwen was equally as passionate about telling everyone how she felt:

"Suddenly Single has made me see that I wasn't living the way I wanted to, I wasn't being true to myself. It helped me stop postponing a lot of things that are dear to me. I always used to consider myself strong and capable, but that wasn't how I was behaving; I needed to Take Charge. Suddenly Single helped me focus on 10 questions and

acknowledge and appreciate my life and my achievements. I now have a positive internal focus for producing results and achieving my goals. I have found meditation a wonderful way to quieten the voices of fear, anxiety, worry and other negative emotions.

"The Little Wins have helped build my confidence, positivity and reinforce my natural desire to feel successful.

"Roy would be proud of how far I have come. I now have a lifestyle that we had both worked hard to achieve.

"Lifestyle is what people want to enjoy. Lifestyle is what people want to maintain and improve, and I feel that I have totally taken charge of mine."

Mary and Gwen considered the Happy, Healthy, Wealthy and Wise Scale.

Take Off

Let's take one more look at the HHWW scale.

HAPPY – You've made it! You're back in control and can see a happy future. You know how to experience 'Your Best Year Yet'.

HEALTHY – You feel amazing and have reached Stage 6 on the Journey of Change. You have regained your self-esteem, feel empowered and secure.

WEALTHY – You understand the truth about money, are better organised financially and free from financial worries.

WISE – You have become a wise woman.

How is your score looking now?

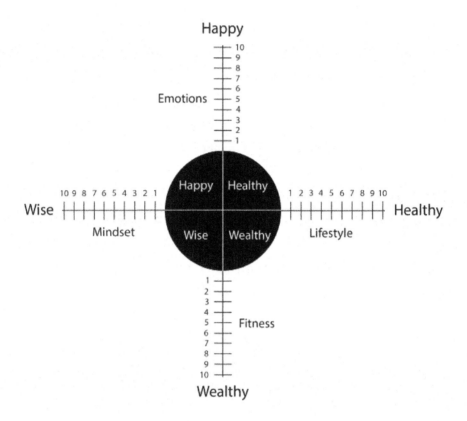

Both Mary and Gwen agreed that they had made large improvements and were now 10 out of 10 on all the scales

Happy

Healthy

Wealthy

Wise

As a Suddenly Single woman, you can now surge forward in an unending unfolding of new challenges, new opportunities, new options, and new discoveries.

You have now completed the Suddenly Single Journey.

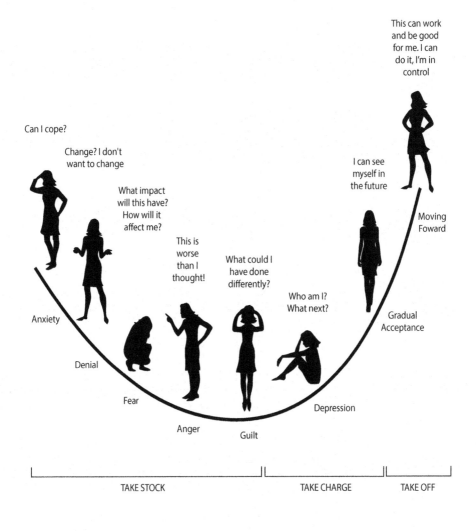

Enjoy...

"My interest is in the future because I am going to spend the rest of my life there."

Charles Kettering

www.suddenly-single.co.uk